The Pathway of
Happiness
Cherish Life and Live Nobly

By Dr. Patrick Hunt

The Pathway of
Happiness

Cherish Life and Live Nobly

Copyright © 2020 by

Dr. Patrick Hunt

ISBN: 978-0-578-71153-9

The Pathway of Happiness: Cherish Life and Live Nobly is written to encourage the young and old to cherish God's gift of life and to live nobly. The purpose of the copyright is to prevent the reproduction, misuse, and abuse of the material. Please address all requests for information or permission to: Dr. Patrick Hunt

M2E Motivational Consulting LLC
Patrick.Hunt@Higherplace.net

Dedication

To all those who have cherished life and lived nobly to help others during the COVID-19 pandemic.

CONTENTS

Acknowledgements

Thanks are given to family and friends who encouraged me in the publication of this book. A special thank you is given to my wife, Terry, for her editorial assistance. Gratitude is expressed to Dr. Denny Bates for assistance in getting this book onto Amazon KDP.

FOREWORD

By Dr. Denny Bates

I personally, know what it means to cherish life. On July 3, 1998, at age 41, I had a massive heart attack. It announced to me just how very fragile life can be. From that time forward, I have made a deliberate choice to never take life for granted again. Life -- I cherish it.

I have come to learn that the pathway of happiness is a journey that is not only a "good idea," but it is God's best idea for you. But therein lies the challenge: how does one get there . . . and remain there? We must make a choice.

The experience of life is filled with daily choices that will lead to distinctive paths. But in making the best choices and taking the best paths, how do you see the options available, to you, the reader? I've come to believe that experience is not the *best* way forward to success. I believe *guided experience* is the most effective way. Fortunately, Dr. Patrick Hunt is an excellent guide. His compass is the Scriptures of the Bible. Jesus, the Light of the world, pierces even the darkest path. "Pat" has laid out a clear course of action as he invites the reader not to only hear about the pathway of happiness, but he shows you how it is possible to make the right choices that will lead you along the path.

The Pathway of Happiness: Cherish Life and Live Nobly is a treasured guidebook that is equally thought provoking and practical. Doctor Hunt has placed his focus on two essential keys for the best experience on the pathway of happiness. In his own words,

I believe life must be cherished and

lived nobly. When we do these two things, we walk on the pathway of happiness. It is my sincere. hope that this book will help you find that pathway for your life.

Pat has done his fine work by carefully writing this book so that it will encourage and lead you. Now, it's time for you to get to work and begin to put into practice these timeless principles as you learn what it's like to live on the pathway of happiness.

Denny Bates, DMin (Leadership)

Writer, Quality Life Coach, and Story Coach

www.ReallyGoodDay4U.com

Preface

The great galvanizing force for the writing of this book was preserving life – especially for veterans and teens. While my immediate family has been spared from the horrible tragedy of suicide, it has been all around me. My first cousin was one of the numerous Vietnam veterans who committed suicide. These tragedies were in my granddaughters' high school, my church, and my workplace.

The actual writing of the book came from my desire to write both hopeful and helpful materials concerning life and Christianity. I desired to write about light rather than darkness. Accordingly, I first wrote about receiving Christ; he is the light of the world. Then I wrote about noble service and the pursuit of true happiness. They both emanate from Christ and the Holy Spirit.

The first chapter entitled *Life-Sustaining Hope* was written to provide reasons for hope. It also provided examples of individuals who overcame horrible situations to live lives that had positive global impacts. I tried to emphasize the reasons for hope, trust in Christ, and the long view of life. The second chapter of this book entitled *Avoid Death – Cherish Life* was written to be a direct and urgent warning against suicides and senseless murders.

I visualized it as the screaming at a child that was about to run into traffic. The last chapter, *The Call of Jesus*, came to me in verse and rhythm over a two-year period of time. It reflects on the Christian life from salvation into eternity.

Overall, this book was written from my profound understanding that life is a precious gift from God. I came to this understanding through the living of more than 70 years. During that time, I have interacted with people across the United States and the world. I have learned lessons from people whose professions ranged from workers in my grandfather's sawmill to chairmen of major corporations. I have also been blessed to have many friends who were preachers, professors, and licensed professionals. Moreover, my tour as an army officer taught me: 1) to understand that the cost of freedom is high and 2) to respect those who served before and after me. My mother and father (a purple-heart veteran of WW II) taught me to strive to be both accomplished and honorable. They also taught me to be diligent and compassionate. My dear wife of more than 50 years taught me much about kindness. Thus, I believe life must be cherished and lived nobly. When we do these two things, we walk on the pathway of happiness. It is my sincere hope that this book will help you find that pathway for your life.

Introduction

At the time you open this book, your pathway may be going through beautiful spring flowers. On the other hand, it may be going through icy and dangerous mountain passes. In either case, your pathway can be one of happiness. Even if this happiness is only in the mind and spirit, the opportunity to be happy is yours.

Together, we will visit and learn insights from many books, places, and people. Among them will be John Milton's poems, the Holocaust prison, and wise King Solomon. From these we will gain hope, insights, and fortified happiness. Additionally, the referenced biblical scriptures will guide you as they did Washington, Lincoln, and King.

Most importantly, we will explore how cherishing life and living nobly allows our pathways to be filled with hope and happiness. So, let us begin with the beginning of the United States of America.

It began with one of the great documents of human history -- the Declaration of Independence. It contains these beautiful words: *We hold these truths to be self-evident, that all men are created equal, that they are endowed by their Creator with certain unalienable rights that among these are life, liberty, and the pursuit of happiness.* The right to life is the premier and essential right! The second two rights are meaningless without the first – life. In other words, for there to be any meaning to liberty or the pursuit of happiness, it is essential that one be alive. It logically follows that life must be cherished.

Life for most people is just taken for granted.   This changes only in times of danger.   Then, life quickly becomes very precious and cherished. If nothing else, the danger and death toll associated with the global pandemic of COVID-19 have made it abundantly clear that life is tenuous. Thus, it should be cherished each and every day. Thankfully, there are countless numbers of people who do cherish life; they provide acts of heroism and mercy every single day.

Unfortunately, in the United States of America there has also been a grave national problem with the lack of appreciation for all human life. We see the fruit of this cheap-life thinking in the horrific homicide statistics. These senseless murders are devastating to families, communities, and our nation. They have created an ocean of tears and shattered lives.

Equally tragic is the frequency of suicides in the young. Many of these children died thinking they were ugly ducklings; they were too young to realize they could become beautiful swans. Suicides are also alarmingly

3

high in the ranks of veterans and active duty military personnel. The military suicides are doubly tragic because: 1) these individuals are the ones who have served and are serving our nation to preserve the rights of life, liberty, and the pursuit of happiness for their fellow citizens; and 2) they are robbing themselves of the most precious right – life.

There are myriad causes for these murders and suicides, including mental illness. There are also laudable efforts to reduce both of these tragedies. The purpose of this book is to be a beacon pointing to the bedrock truth that life is precious: It is to be cherished even when the circumstances of life are extremely difficult.

Let there be no doubt, the circumstances of life in 2020 were difficult. They were difficult in three simultaneously challenging areas: There were great challenges from COVID-19 health dangers, from extreme social tensions, and from financial devastations.

In response, this book provides the basis for cherishing life and maintaining a life-sustaining hope. It is Christian in nature; it emphasizes the good news that eternal life is available. This everlasting life is above all to be grasped and valued: Both our present life and our eternal life are inalienable and precious gifts from God our creator.

Relative to the inalienable right of liberty, people in the Western world are largely at liberty to live their lives free of oppression. Enslavement is generally in the form of sin and addictions that range from drugs to gambling. Unfortunately, liberty is not available for much of humanity. While liberty is precious and important, it is not the focus of this book other than to stress that everyone has the ultimate freedom to choose how they think.

Relative to the pursuit of happiness, this book emphasizes living nobly to the benefit of ourselves, our neighbors, and our posterity. Noble living is a time-tested pathway of happiness.

In contrast, ignoble living is a well proven pathway to misery and death. It is characterized by hedonism, debauchery, and narcissism. Its fruits are violence, destruction, and death. We have seen ignoble living's hideous face revealed in the vile murder of George Floyd.

Let every American commit to live out the dream written by Samuel Francis Smith in the lyrics of *My Country, 'Tis of Thee*. Let us resolve to truly be *the land of the noble free*.

Fortunately, we have seen multitudes of people living out this nobility with great and small contributions that preserve life. We have seen it with the doctors, nurses, and EMS personnel on the front lines of the

COVID-19 pandemic. We have seen it in the efforts of truck drivers delivering essential goods under difficult conditions. We also have seen noble living in the grocery stores and drugstores where pharmacists, stockers, and cashiers have been potentially exposed to COVID-19 every day. Equally, important but unseen are the enormous efforts of the industries that make critical deliveries possible. For instance, there have been great efforts extended to manufacture and provide the containers for disinfectants. Most importantly, we all have the opportunity to live honorably. Every person can make principled choices each day. Let us choose to cherish life and live nobly each day.

Chapter 2

Life-Sustaining Hope

This chapter is meant to provide hope -- not just temporary hope. It is intended to provide a life-sustaining hope. This hope is and has been desperately needed for teens, young adults, and veterans. Additionally, it is now needed as people deal with the overwhelming stresses of a rapidly changing world.

Fortunately, there is great news: *Help Can Be Obtained and Hope Can Be Restored*. While there are no perfect ways or perfect people, there is perfect love. It is communicated in the living words of the Bible. It is also described in song by Charles Wesley as *Love divine, all loves excelling, joy of heaven to earth come down*. This perfect love removes fear and restores hope. Moreover, it provides a <u>Life-Sustaining Hope</u>. Both this love and hope are communicated in countless Christian songs. One such song is the beautiful *Whispering Hope* written by Jim Reeves. Its comforting lyrics contain the following verse: *Hope with a gentle persuasion whispers a comforting word.* The most comforting words are that we are everlastingly loved by Jesus Christ, the Redeemer; He died to redeem us. Moreover, He arose from the dead and conquered sin and death. In knowing Him, millions have been transformed from hopelessness to live wonderful and fulfilled lives. This God-given transformation allowed Max Lucado to write his book *Unshakable Hope.* This transformation also inspired John Newton to write the powerful song *Amazing Grace.* It contains this most comforting verse: *Through many dangers, toils, and snares I have already come. 'Tis Grace hath brought me safe thus far and Grace will lead me home.*

Great People Who Grasped Hope

Let us consider four people whose lives were saved by the power of life-sustaining hope and trust in God.

First, let us consider Dr. Viktor Frankl, who was delivered from Hitler's Holocaust prisons. Frankl was an Austrian psychiatry professor at the time of the Nazi Holocaust. To the Nazis, it made no difference that he was a gifted teacher and doctor. He was simply another Jew. Accordingly, he was sent to the prisons and extermination camps. This reality thrust Dr. Frankl into an all-consuming struggle to simply survive each day and to find relief from unimaginable suffering. This was suffering and torment at all levels of existence: Suffering that few have ever known. Moreover, his entire family was lost during the Holocaust.

Yet, he clung to a life-sustaining hope. He did this by focusing his thoughts on his beloved wife and his God. Moreover, he found that no matter what the circumstances, he could choose what he thought. This allowed him freedom in his mind while his body was in prison and in great pain. After the whole ghastly holocaust experience was over, he lived a fulfilled life in which he helped millions find meaning in their lives. He recorded this experience in his book *Man's Search For Meaning*.

For our second person who found life-sustaining hope, we will consider Joseph. His life is recorded in the Biblical book of Genesis. He lived in ancient Egypt and the land of Canaan. As a young boy in Canaan, he was the favored son of his father Jacob and his mother Rachel. At a young age, Joseph had prophetic dreams. His dreams symbolized that his entire family would bow before him. Now, Joseph had older brothers born to his father by his wife Leah and the maidservants of both Leah and Rachel. Because of his dreams and his favored status, he was hated by these brothers. Thus, on an occasion when Joseph was far away from his father, his brothers bound him and sold him into slavery in Egypt. They then told his father that Joseph had been killed by a wild beast. Jacob mourned the loss of this son with an everlasting sorrow. His only comfort was that he had Benjamin. He was the only other son of Rachel, and Joseph's younger brother.

Meanwhile, Joseph was alone in Egypt; he had become the slave of Pharaoh's captain of the guard, Potiphar. Even so, God's providential favor was upon Joseph. The Lord blessed all his endeavors, and he was soon in charge of everything for Potiphar. He was his chief of staff. For a short time, things were looking up for Joseph. However, Joseph was a strikingly handsome young man, and Potiphar's wife tried to seduce him, but

Joseph wanted nothing to do with her. He honored the kindness that Potiphar had bestowed upon him. Nonetheless, this disgraceful woman was not finished with Joseph, and one day when Joseph rebuffed her advances she decided to scream and accuse him of attacking her. Upon hearing this lie, Potiphar was furious and threw Joseph into jail. So now, Joseph had moved from being a slave to being an imprisoned slave. Nonetheless, God blessed Joseph in jail, and soon he was in charge of the prisoners. Moreover, he was able to interpret prophetic dreams. He even interpreted a dream for Pharaoh's cupbearer. He asked the cupbearer to appeal to Pharaoh on his behalf. The cupbearer assured him that he would make this appeal, but he forgot Joseph.

Two full years after interpreting the cupbearer's dream Joseph was to see God's providential timing when Pharaoh had a most terrible dream. Pharaoh was extremely distressed. Yet, no one in the land could interpret the dream. Then, the cup bearer remembered Joseph, and he told Pharaoh that there was a prisoner who could interpret dreams exactly as they would be fulfilled. Joseph was swiftly brought to Pharaoh. He then revealed the dream's meaning to Pharaoh. He told him that the dream foretold seven years of plentiful production within the land that would be followed by seven years of severe famine. The famine would be so severe that it would consume all the productivity of the bounteous years. Joseph also told Pharaoh that 1) God was firmly warning him and 2) he should store provisions from the plentiful years to sustain the land of Egypt during the famine. Pharaoh believed the interpretation, and he favored Joseph's plan. He then put Joseph in charge of everything in Egypt. Thus, Joseph was Lord of Egypt -- second only to Pharaoh. Everyone bowed before him. During the good years,

Joseph built storage facilities and stored enormous quantities of grain. Then the good years were gone like the wind, and the full force of the famine descended on Egypt and the surrounding countries including Canaan.

In Canaan, Jacob had learned that there was food in Egypt. He instructed his sons to go and buy food so that the entire family would not starve. Accordingly, the brothers that sold Joseph into slavery traveled and arrived in Egypt. There they bowed before Joseph – just as foretold in Joseph's boyhood dream. They did not recognize Joseph, but he recognized them immediately. Joseph agreed to sell them grain, but he set up a test to see if they were still dishonorable before his father and his younger brother, Benjamin. At the end of the test, he presented them with the claim that Benjamin had been found to be a thief. Moreover, he would be imprisoned in Egypt while the other brothers could return home to their father. However, the brothers had changed, and they pleaded for Benjamin's release. Judah even offered to exchange himself as the slave for Benjamin so that his father would not lose his only son born to his beloved wife Rachel.

At this time, Joseph revealed himself to his brothers and said to them: *you meant it for evil, but God meant it for good. He sent me ahead to prepare for you so that you would not perish during the famine.* He then told them to bring his father and the entire family to him quickly and that he would care for them in Egypt. The family did come to him, and they all prospered during Joseph's entire life. Moreover, Joseph was forever remembered and honored. Thus, in the account of Joseph we see an example of the providential hand of God working out the affairs of men.

This truth of God's providential sovereignty is presented by the apostle Paul in the book of Romans. It is powerfully stated in Romans 8:28. *And we know that in all things God works for the good of those who love him, who have been called according to his purpose.* This is a bedrock truth upon which countless men and women have withstood the storms of life.

A modern-day version of this story was when the proud and guilty Chuck Colson (President Nixon's Watergate crew) was placed in prison. Colson detailed this experience in his book, *Born Again.* Even though he was guilty, God was providentially working in his life. Colson was a new, born-again believer when he entered prison, but he emerged from prison with a profound desire to help prisoners by communicating the good news of the Christian gospel. Colson spent his entire life communicating the gospel to the world with his ever-present special emphasis on his global Prison Fellowship ministry. He understood that God had put him through trials to prepare him for a noble work that would define his life. We can all reach out from our conditions of despair and trust in God's providential hand. We can also look for what noble endeavors that He may have planned for our future. Examples of fourteen noble lives are presented in two books: *Seven Men and the secret of their Greatness* along with *Seven Women and the secret of their Greatness both* by Eric Metaxas.

A fourth, inspiring story of restored hope is that of Joni Eareckson Tada. She is different from the previous three examples because she was never delivered from the damage of her accident. At the age of 18, she had a diving accident that left her a quadriplegic. While she initially struggled with depression and suicidal thoughts, she found hope, strength, and purpose in Christ. For decades she has had a global Christian ministry called Joni and Friends. She is married, writes books, does artwork, sings beautifully, and prays fervently. Accordingly, she is a global ambassador for life-sustaining hope and the value of each life. Let us all be such noble ambassadors. Let us all trust in God, fortify hope, and cherish life.

Hope for Everyone

If you, a loved one, or a friend is struggling with hopelessness, know that perfect love and hope are there for every living person. Christ left us with these comforting words – *I came that they may have life and have it to the full.* Trust Christ and wait on his providential care; He will provide life-sustaining hope, a song for your heart, and the abundant life.

Supporting Scripture

Proverbs 24:11 – Rescue those being led away to death; hold back those staggering towards slaughter.

Psalm 139:14 – I praise you because I am fearfully and wonderfully made.

John 10:10 – I came that they may have life and have it to the full.

1 John 4:18 -- There is no fear in love. But perfect love drives out fear.

John 14:19 – because I live you also will   live.

Psalm 23:4 Even though I walk through the darkest valley, I will fear no evil, for you are with me; your rod and your staff, they comfort me.

Joshua 1:9 Have I not commanded you? Be strong and courageous. Do not be afraid; do not be discouraged, for the Lord your God will be with you wherever you go."

Jeremiah 29:11 -- For I know the plans I have for you," declares the LORD, "plans to prosper you and not to harm you, plans to give you hope and a future.

Chapter 3

Avoid Death -- Cherish Life

At critical points of life, a slight nudge can be lifesaving or catastrophic. Many have lived lives of condemnation and recrimination for words and actions that nudged another person into a horrible act. Be careful that your words and actions do not crush another person's spirit. Be alert and aware that a kind and encouraging word has pulled many from the edge of despair and destruction.

We are going to consider six life banners. I implore you to read them slowly, deliberately, and seriously. Please grasp the power of the last line of each banner – With life there is hope.

The following is a brief recounting of a lady I knew professionally. She smothered hope and committed murder: All hope was extinguished. She had been acting out fits of anger and violence. Then in a blind rage she killed her husband, their young child, and herself. All hope was gone. She could have chosen numerous other courses of action that would have allow life to evolve into happiness. She could have found life-sustaining hope like our champions of the previous chapter. Let us resolve to do differently. Let us resolve to cherish life and live nobly.

Now, let us consider the six:

LIFESAVING-BANNERS.

If one were ever to consider death because of cruelty or deprivation,

STOP: Avoid Death – Cherish Life.

<u>With Life There Is Hope!</u>

If one were ever to consider death because of abusive parents or bullying,

STOP: Avoid Death – Cherish Life.

<u>With Life There Is Hope!</u>

If one were ever to consider death because of a wrecked career, a shattered relationship, or a lost loved one,

STOP: Avoid Death – Cherish Life.

With Life There Is Hope!

If one were ever to consider the death of another person because of seething anger, rage, or simple inconvenience,

STOP: Avoid Death – Cherish Life.

With Life There Is Hope!

If one were ever to flirt with death

because of careless life habits,

drugs, or dangerous associates,

STOP: Avoid Death – Cherish Life.

<u>With Life There Is Hope!</u>

If one were ever to consider or flirt with death because of any reason,

STOP: Avoid Death – Cherish Life.

<u>With Life There Is Hope!</u>

Supporting Scripture

Psalm 34:18 -- The Lord is close to the brokenhearted and saves those who are crushed in spirit.

John 10:10 – I came that they may have life, and have it abundantly.

Psalm 139:14 – I praise you because I am fearfully and wonderfully made.

Genesis 4:10 --The Lord said, "What have you done? Listen! Your brother's blood cries out to me from the ground."

Proverbs 1:18 -- These men lie in wait for their own blood; they ambush only themselves!

Proverbs 29:11 -- A fool gives full vent to his anger, but a wise man keeps himself under control.

Chapter 4

Receive and Cherish Eternal Life

The great truth is that while we should live in peace with people of all faiths, these faiths are often mutually exclusive. The faith that trusts and serves the true God is the only one that matters for eternity. Living with this truth and acting on it requires great intellectual and moral integrity. This integrity is essential to face one inescapable truth: We shall surely die and surely face eternity with our decision about God.

Oh, one may say -- there is neither God nor eternity. Yet, when one reflects on this point of view, it does not seem very reassuring. It denies the vast and amazing order of both the universe and the complexities of life on this earth; it ascribes a lot to random chance. Relative to random chance, it would seem that the state of science at the time of Darwin until about the 1980's conceivably would have allowed for the concept of evolution of the human species on earth. However, the current knowledge of science and the universe requires acknowledgment of a designed order and a creator of this order. The most complete and compelling presentation of this creator is in the God of the Bible.

There we learn that there is heaven to be gained and hell to be avoided. Nonetheless, it is currently popular to believe that everyone is going to heaven. After all, God is love and a loving God would send no one to hell. This position ignores God's perfect justice: God cannot ignore sin. It is important to remember what Christ said: "Enter by the narrow gate, for the gate is wide and the way is easy that leads to destruction, and those who enter by it are many."

The narrow gate is described by John 3:16. "For God so loved the world that he gave his one and only son that whosoever believes in him should not perish but have eternal life."

When we receive eternal life through Jesus Christ, he saves our souls; he also fills us with his Holy Spirit.

Accordingly, we will never walk alone. This is true even if our pathway leads us through the valley of the shadow of death. Christ has promised he will never leave us nor forsake us. We can maintain a life-sustaining hope and trust in his providential and eternal care.

Supporting Scripture

Hebrews 11:6 -- Without faith it is impossible to please God, because anyone who comes to him must believe that he exists and that he rewards those who earnestly seek him.

John 14:6 -- Jesus answered, "I am the way and the truth and the life. No one comes to the Father except through me.

Romans 10:9 --If you declare with your mouth, "Jesus is Lord," and believe in your heart that God raised him from the dead, you will be saved.

John 14: 18 -- I will not leave you comfortless: I will come to you.

1 Corinthians 6: 19 -- Do you not know that your bodies are temples of the Holy Spirit, who is in you, whom you have received from God?

Psalm 23: 4 -- Even though I walk through the darkest valley, I will fear no evil, for you are with me; your rod and your staff, they comfort   me.

Chapter 5

The Greatest Pursuit of Happiness

King Solomon, the son of David the king of Israel, was renowned for being both the wisest and richest man of his time. His Proverbs and sayings continue to have a clarifying effect on how people live wise and productive lives, i.e. noble lives. Among the most beneficial things that can be learned from Solomon are the lessons from the book of Ecclesiastes. Here we see how a rich and wise king endeavored to find the meaning of a life well lived. In his own words he did not limit the desires of his heart. He planted gardens, built palaces, pursued fine music, and enjoyed the company of good friends. He undertook and succeeded in accomplishing great projects. However, he soon realized the emptiness and the vanity of these endeavors. He quickly came to recognize that the ability

34

to truly enjoy one's work along with the fellowship of food and drink was a gift from God.

However, he also realized the vanity lodged within his pursuits. Most vexing to him, a diligent and wise man, was the fact that all his works on earth would be left to another person. He fully realized that this person might be wise and diligent, or they could be a completely foolish sluggard. He also realized that the same fate awaited both the diligent and the slugger -- the grave. When he looked at all his endeavors, he concluded that those endeavors not blessed by God were meaningless: A chasing after the wind. Thus, he says at the end of the book of Ecclesiastes "Let us hear the conclusion of the whole matter: Fear God and keep his commandments: for this is the whole duty of man. For God shall bring every work into judgment, with every secret thing, whether it be good, or whether it be evil".

This could be paraphrased to thank God for your life and eternal salvation then live nobly to his glory.

This conclusion is similar to Viktor Frankl's conclusion that there were only two types of men -- those who chose to live nobly and those who chose to live infamously. After returning home from his Holocaust experience, he had this most liberating realization: He said *the crowning experience of all, for the homecoming man, was the wonderful feeling, after all he had suffered, there was nothing he need fear anymore – except God.*

The great guidance that we get from Solomon's Palace and the Holocaust prison is that there is nothing in this life worth pursuing except serving God and there is nothing to eternally fear except God.

Supporting Scripture

Mark 8: 36 -- For what shall it profit a man, if he shall gain the whole world, and lose his own soul?

Proverbs 23:5 -- Cast but a glance at riches, and they are gone, for they will surely sprout wings and fly off to the sky like an eagle.

Matthew 10: 28 -- Do not be afraid of those who kill the body but can't kill the soul. Instead, be afraid of the one who can destroy both soul and body in hell.

Chapter 6

Noble Living Great or Small

Noble living has been eloquently depicted by poet John Milton. He was a famous English poet of the 17th century. His great passion was noble service for the Lord Jesus Christ. One of his most famous works was *Paradise Lost.* Another was *Paradise Regained.* At the height of his career, Milton had a problem -- he was going blind. This inability hindered the great works he desired to do for the Lord. His reflections on going blind and his inability to write are described in one of his famous poems, *When I Consider How My Light Is Spent.*

This poem has spoken to me for more than 50 years. When I was 17 years old, a senior in high school, we studied this great poem.

The famous closing line of the poem is -- "They also serve who only stand and wait". One night during this period of high school, I had a dream in which the Lord clearly stated to me "Milton has it correct." At that age, the simplicity of the Lord's statement seemed to be obvious. One could live their life to the best of their ability and in accordance with their best understanding of God's will and then rest satisfied with the results. This was very comforting to me because it meant that my best efforts were all that was needed. Like the widow's two mites – all that we have is all that is needed.

When I was 17, I did not even dream that God would allow me to serve him in the area of agricultural and natural resources research. He provided me with magnificent professors and remarkably talented mentors. He guided my career and allowed me to be unusually productive, honored, and blessed.

Now, more than five decades after the dream, I have retired from my professional career. Yet, I still visualize the wonderful things God may allow me to accomplish for his kingdom. Furthermore, I am comforted by the truth so eloquently revealed by Milton's poem. We also serve if we simply stand and wait for the Lord. Moreover, if we pray with expectant faith while we stand and wait, we bring the power of God's throne to the wait.

Supporting Scripture

Luke 21:1-4 -- As Jesus looked up, he saw the rich putting their gifts into the temple treasury. He also saw a poor widow put in two very small copper coins. "Truly I tell you," he said, "this poor widow has put in more than all the others. All these people gave their gifts out of their wealth; but she out of her poverty put in all she had to live on.

Exodus 14:21-22 -- Then Moses stretched out his hand over the sea, and all that night the Lord drove the sea back with a strong east wind and turned it into dry land. The waters were divided, and the Israelites went through the sea on dry ground, with a wall of water on their right and on their left.

Colossians 3:17 -- Whatever you do, whether in word or deed, do it all in the name of the Lord Jesus, giving thanks to God the Father through him.

Chapter 7

The Call of Jesus

I heard the call of Jesus say my child come to me.

I came and then I heard him say receive my gift to thee.

It is the cleansing blood I shed upon Calvary.

And it shall wash and cleanse your soul of all iniquity.

I heard the call of Jesus say Christian come to me.

I came and then I heard him say now Christian follow me.

For I have work for you to do both here and across the sea.

That work was there for you to do before you came to be.

I heard the call of Jesus say Pilgrim come to me.

I came and then I heard him say I am strength to thee.

Even when the road is dark and long I your way will be.

And on the stormy seas of life secure in me you will be.

I heard the call of Jesus say Christian come to me.

I came and then I heard him say my children plead to me.

Lift up the lost and hurting ones for they are dear to me.

And in these faithful acts of love my healing hands you'll be.

I heard the call of Jesus say my child come to me.

I came and then I heard him say you've done your work for me.

Come now receive your royal crown beside the glassy sea.

And there my treasured child you'll be for all eternity.

Author and Publisher: The lyrics were written and published, in 2019, by Dr. Patrick Hunt; all rights are reserved.

The lyrics can be sung to the Kingsford melody of *I heard the voice of Jesus say* – written by Horatius Bonar in 1846.

Supporting Scripture

John 3: 16 -- For God so loved the world that he gave his one and only Son, that whoever believes in him shall not perish but have eternal life.

Ephesians 2:10 -- For we are God's handiwork, created in Christ Jesus to do good works, which God prepared in advance for us to do.

John 14:6 -- Jesus answered, "I am the way and the truth and the life.

Genesis 12:1 -- The LORD had said to Abram, "Go from your country, your people and your father's household to the land I will show you.

Matthew 25:40 -- The King will reply, 'Truly I tell you, whatever you did for one of the least of these brothers and sisters of mine, you did for me

Mathew 25:23 -- His master replied, 'Well done, good and faithful servant! You have been faithful with a few things; I will put you in charge of many things. Come and share your master's happiness.

Chapter 8

Epilogue

We started the journey through this book by declaring that the pathway of your life can be a pathway of happiness. Even if this happiness is only in the mind and spirit, the opportunity to be happy is yours. We stated that the power of biblical scripture could guide you as it had guided Washington, Lincoln, and King.

We then discussed the priceless and inalienable rights declared in the Declaration of Independence: life, liberty, and the pursuit of happiness. The focus was on life because the other two rights are meaningless without life. While extremely important, liberty was not a focus of this book. The reader was encouraged to pursue happiness through noble living.

To facilitate the cherishing of life, we discussed life-sustaining hope. There we featured songs, books, and life examples that support hope. One might call these examples of hope, Viktor Frankl, Joseph, Charles Colson, and Joni Erickson Tada heroes and heroines of hope. We then considered six life banners that emphasized avoiding death and cherishing life.

The book then moved from physical life to the need for eternal life. A rationale was presented for believing the truth of an eternal existence and God's judgement. Moreover, there was Christ's warning against drifting down the broad road to destruction. There was also an affirmation of the Christian beliefs for receiving eternal life.

Relative to happiness, we examined the life of Solomon and his pursuit of happiness. It is described in the Bible in the book of Ecclesiastes. We closed this chapter by comparing Solomon's conclusions about life to those of Viktor Frankl's after his Holocaust experience. This led to the awesome conclusion that there was nothing in this life worth pursuing except serving God and there was nothing to eternally fear except God.

We then considered noble living both great and small. We used John Milton's famous poem *When I Consider How My Light Is Spent*. The liberating idea presented by Milton and discussed in this chapter is that our noble service may be great like Moses or small like the widow's two mites – all that we have is all that is needed.

The Christian life was presented in chapter 7 in poetic form and hymn lyrics for *The Call of Jesus*. It encompasses salvation, service, and our eternal home with God.

The hope is that after reading this book you are in a higher place in your thinking, in your heart, and in your soul relative to your present and eternal life. It is also hoped that it is evident that true happiness is found in noble service and living, whether that service be great or small. Moreover, it is hoped that you are now better equipped and motivated 1) to communicate the wonder of life, 2) to shout to the world that life is to be cherished, and 3) to demonstrate noble living to the glory of God and the benefit of you, your neighbors, and your posterity.

Shout that life is to be cherished when you wake in the morning, and then praise God that you are alive. Communicate that life is to be cherished in the way you walk and talk. Communicate that life is to be cherished in the way you overlook the imperfections in your family and your neighbors. Communicate that life is to be cherished in the way you kiss babies, the way you frolic with children, and the way you celebrate years of life with the elderly. Live nobly and cherish each moment of life.

Finally, lift up the lost and hurting ones. Be a beacon to God's eternal life through Jesus Christ.

Shout, sing, and rejoice in the truth that you will be able to cherish your eternal life in God's presence for all eternity.

Bibliography

1. Clark, Kenneth S. *Stories of America's greatest songs,* 4th ed. New York: National Bureau for the Advancement of Music, 1941. *Call number:* ML3551 .C5 1941.

2. Colson, Charles W. *Born Again.* Grand Rapids: Chosen – a division of Baker Publishing Group. 2008. Print. p383.

3. Frankl, Viktor E. *Man's Search for Meaning.* Forward by Harold S. Kushner. Boston: Beacon Press. 2006. Print. p165.

4. Lucado, Max. *Unshakable Hope.* Nashville: Thomas Nelson. 2018. Print. p216.

5. Metaxas, Eric. *Seven Men and The Secret of Their Greatness.* Nashville: Thomas Nelson. 2015. Print. p244.

6.   Metaxas, Eric. Seven Women and The Secret of Their Greatness Nashville: Thomas Nelson. 2015. Print. p240

7.   Milton, John (1608-1674). *Paradise Lost and Paradise Regained.* Lawrence: 2006. Print. p136.

8.   All scripture citations are from the NIV 11 translation and are used under the Gratis Use Guidelines of Zondervan. Grand Rapids, MI.

Meet Dr. Patrick Hunt

D r. Patrick Hunt grew up in North Carolina where his mother's family had lived for over 250 years. It was from his family and their Presbyterian Church that his character, imagination, and dreams were formed. The community of his childhood was also the community of his wife. They have been soulmates on this journey of life for over 50 years.

Dr. Hunt started his education with a bachelor's degree from Clemson

University. He then received his PhD from the University of Florida. After receiving his PhD, he served a tour in the U.S. Army. At the time of his discharge, he was a captain. He holds in highest regard the men and women with whom he served.

He has a great love for research and development. He retired after a distinguished forty-year career as an agricultural scientist. There he published more than 150 peer reviewed scientific papers. He is a Fellow of four scientific societies.

Throughout his career his wife and family were always a priority. He and his wife were involved in their children's activities, dreams, and character development. They are similarly involved in the lives of their grandchildren.

Dr. Hunt is now involved in the exhortation and encouragement of both children and adults. He writes and speaks to encourage everyone to cherish life and live nobly.

He is hopeful that the materials on his website (drpatrickhunt.com) along with his books will be both comforting and inspirational.

Other books published
by Dr. Patrick Hunt
Available on Amazon.com

LIFE-SUSTAINING
HOPE

DR. PATRICK HUNT

Matthew 11: 28-30 -- Come to me, all you who are weary and burdened, and I will give you rest. Take my yoke upon you and learn from me, for I am gentle and humble in heart, and you will find rest for your souls. For my yoke is easy and my burden is light.

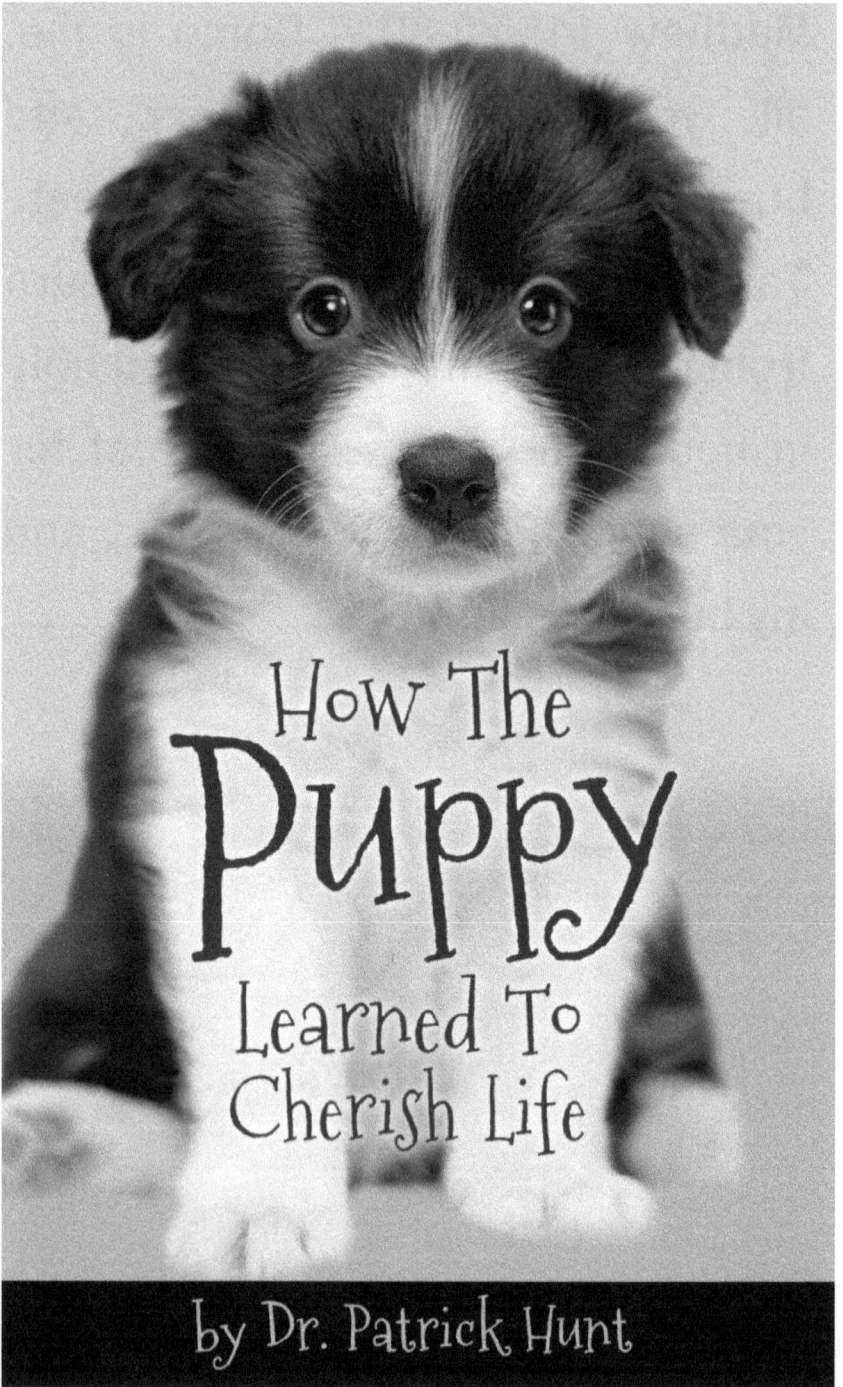

How The
Puppy
Learned To
Cherish Life

by Dr. Patrick Hunt

Matthew 19:14 -- Jesus said, "Let the little children come to me, and do not hinder them, for the kingdom of heaven belongs to such as these.

www.ingramcontent.com/pod-product-compliance
Lightning Source LLC
Chambersburg PA
CBHW022128280326
41933CB00007B/594